Zargon Zoo

Paul Shipton

HEINEMANN NEW WAVE READERS

After many days the space ship arrived at the planet.

Computer, what do you know about this planet?

It is the third planet from the sun. It is called Earth.

2

Go closer, please, Computer.
Earth people live in houses. Many houses together are called towns or cities.

Very interesting. Show us some Earth people.
These are young Earth people— teenagers.
They're ugly, aren't they? They look terrible.
Yes! Let's take this one.

Grantford was a small town in the North of England. It had schools, shops, offices and parks. It was a nice quiet town... but it was boring. Phil Naylor and his friends lived there. Today they were bored. They were always bored.
Let's go to the cinema.
No, we went to the cinema yesterday.
Let's play football.
We can't. You lost the ball!
Well, I'm going home. I've got to do my homework.

It was five o'clock. Phil started to walk home. He didn't like homework, but tonight he had lots of homework.
I'm so bored. Grantford is so boring. It's so bor-
ZAP

When Phil opened his eyes, he was in a strange room. In front of him he saw two very strange creatures.

"I was right. Earth people are so ugly."

"Help! What's happening?"

"Hello."

"Um, hello. Wh-where am I? And... who are you? WHAT are you?"

The first creature spoke.

"We are Zargons. We come from a planet far away from Earth. We don't think you can say our real names, but you can call us Jim and Tony. Welcome to planet Zarg, Earth person."

For the first time an Earth person met a Zargon. They shook hands.

"Well, this isn't boring. And it's better than doing homework."

"We want to know more about your planet. What are these things? Please tell us."

The Zargon touched the computer. Suddenly there were three things in front of Phil.

"This is a TV. People watch TV."

"This is a gun. Be careful! It's dangerous."

"This is a tennis racquet."

"Is it dangerous?"

"No! Tennis is a sport."

"Thank you. We want to ask you some more questions."

Phil sat down. The Zargons began to ask more questions.

"What do you know about computers?"

"Um, I like playing computer games."

"Now tell us about cars."

"I haven't got a car, because I'm only 14. I've got a bicycle."

"This is a very stupid Earth person."

The Zargons asked hundreds of questions. Phil didn't know any answers.

The Zargons discussed Phil's answers.
Hmm. Earth people are interesting. They live in houses, they watch TV, they speak different languages. There are two kinds of Earth people – women and men.
What is this one?
A young man. He is 14 years old in Earth time. He doesn't know much about Earth things.
Phil stood up.
I'm sorry, but I've got to go home now. It's nearly dinner time. Before I go, please tell me – are you the leaders of the Planet Zarg?
No, we are the directors of the Zargon Zoo. You are in the biggest and best zoo in the universe.
Their ears were orange, because they were happy and proud. They loved their Zoo.
Great! I love zoos. Can I see the animals? Please. Can I?
I don't think you understand, Earth person. You are one of the animals.
This room is your cage. You can't leave.

That night Phil couldn't sleep. He was alone and afraid. He wanted to be home in Grantford. In the morning the Zargons returned.

"Good morning. Tomorrow everyone on Zarg is coming to see our new animal—you! We must prepare you for tomorrow. Our computer knows all about Earth clothes."

The Zargon touched a button on the computer and Phil's clothes changed.

First he wore cowboy clothes.

Then he wore a suit and bowler hat.

"The computer saw these clothes on TV."

"Too old-fashioned, I think."

"I like the suit. What is he holding?"

"It's called an 'umbrella'. I don't know how it works."

"Perhaps it's dangerous."

en a pop star's clothes.
o you
ke his
nglasses?
Yes, but why is he wearing sunglasses? There's no sun.
Finally Phil wore his clothes again.
I think these clothes are best.
I think Earth clothes are great!

Then the Zargons brought some things from Earth into the room. A telephone — but it didn't work. Some records — but there was no record player. A fridge — but there was nothing in it. A pair of football boots — but there was no football. A TV — but it showed only cowboy films.

"I don't like cowboy films."

"Excellent. Now the people of Zarg can come and see him."

They put up advertisements for the zoo all over Zarg.

Come and see the EARTH BOY. He is the ugliest creature in the universe. It's incredible — he's got FIVE FINGERS! He's got HAIR on his HEAD! He eats dead animals. He watches a strange box called 'TV'. Come to the zoo now. The Earth boy is waiting for you. (Entrance only 4 splots*)

*1 splot = £2

"I heard Earth people are blue."

"I hope he's watching TV."

"How many legs have Earth people got?"

Soon the Zargons began to arrive. They all wanted to see the zoo's new animal — the Earth boy. They paid their money and went to the window of Phil's cage. They were all excited so their ears were red.

10

Hundreds of eyes looked at Phil. He didn't look back at them. He watched television.

"Here is the Earth boy. Earth people are strong, but they are not very intelligent."

"Wow!"

"Look at his ears!"

"The Earth boy is now going to eat dinner."

A small door opened. A hand pushed Phil's dinner into the room.

The round thing is a 'beefburger'. It is the meat of another Earth animal — a cow. The small green things are called 'peas'. The other things are 'chips'. Earth people eat with a knife and fork.

The crowd loved dinner time.

All the Zargons laughed.

I don't like peas!

When all the Zargons left, Phil was alone. The television was quiet.

"Look! He's eating it!"

"It's disgusting."

"HA! HA! HA!"

"YUK!"

I've got to escape.

Phil waited. His eyes were closed, but he wasn't asleep. At last the food door opened. A Zargon hand pushed the last meal of the day into the room.

Now!

Phil jumped up quickly. He grabbed the Zargon's hand and pulled him into the room. The Zargon fell over. His ears were blue, because he was afraid. Phil pushed himself through the food door.

He was in a long corridor.

Which way do I go? Right? Left? This way!

He could hear the Zargon alarm.

WARNING! THE EARTH BOY IS ESCAPING! WARNING! HE IS STRONG AND DANGEROUS. WARNING!

Phil came to three doors.

Which door?

12

He ran through the door on the left. The room was another cage in the zoo. Inside there was another creature. It was blue and it had no legs. It was VERY big! In fact it was ENORMOUS!

"Hi! My name is Van. Who are you?"

"I'm Phil. I come from Earth. I'm trying to escape from this place."

"Hey Phil, relax. Sit down. Have a glass of oil. It's the best drink in the universe. I drink 50 litres a day. So what's the problem Phil? Why are you running?"

"I come from Earth. My town is called Grantford. I know it's boring, but it's my home and I love it. This zoo is wrong. I need freedom. I WANT TO BE FREE!"

The Zargons listened in the next room.

I WANT TO BE FREE!

The two Zargons entered the room. Their ears were green because they were sad.

Earth boy, we heard everything. You want to be free. We didn't know that. The other animals are happy here, because they've got everything they want.

I'm happy here. Does anyone want a glass of oil?

But Earth people are different. You need to be free. You Earth people are sometimes dangerous and stupid, but you've got good hearts. We can't keep you here. Goodbye Phil Naylor and good luck.

14

Good--bye.

ZAP

Phil was back in Grantford. He looked at his watch. The time was exactly the same - five o'clock. Phil looked around - trees, houses, cars, EARTH! It was great to be home. He ran to his friends.

Hi, Phil. Where did you go?

Er... umm.

Nobody is going to believe me.

Everything was the same.

So, what are we going to do?

Let's go swimming.

No, I've got an idea. Let's go to the zoo.

NO!

Heinemann International

A division of Heinemann Educational Books Ltd
Halley Court, Jordan Hill, Oxford OX2 8EJ

OXFORD   LONDON   EDINBURGH
MADRID   PARIS   ATHENS   BOLOGNA
MELBOURNE   SYDNEY   AUCKLAND   SINGAPORE   TOKYO
IBADAN   NAIROBI   GABORONE   HARARE
PORTSMOUTH(NH)

ISBN 0 435 27727 8

This reader is also available on cassette
ISBN 0 435 27833 9

© Paul Shipton, 1991
First published 1991

All rights reserved; no part of this publication may be reproduced, stored in a retrieval system, or transmitted in any form or by any means, electronic, mechanical, photocopying, recording, or otherwise, without the prior written permission of the Publishers.

Designed by Threefold Design
Illustrations by Martin Chatterton

Typeset by Threefold Design
Printed and bound in Spain by Printeksa

HEINEMANN NEW WAVE READERS
Series Editor: Alan C. McLean
Level 2

Double Danger *by Tony Hopwood*
Karateka *by Sue Leather and Marje Brash*
Kate's Revenge *by Philip Prowse*
Zargon Zoo *by Paul Shipton*

---

91 92 93 94 95 96 10 9 8 7 6 5 4 3 2 1